The Guide to Balancing
Chaos & Career

VOLUME I

T.M.B.

Copyright © 2017 T.M.B.

All rights reserved.

ISBN: 1976215269
ISBN-13: 978-1976215261

DEDICATION

φ

To my loving mother, thank you for embodying hard work and grace. To my past, thank you for the lessons. To my future self, may you look back on your accomplishments and find motivation. Finally, to my readers, thank you for entrusting my creation with your mind and allowing my perspective on life to intertwine with yours.

CONTENTS

Forward   *i*
How to Use This Guide   *ii*

Part One: Making the Decision
1   The Big Vent   1
2   Self-Blaming   10
3   Your Life is Worth Living   17

Part Two: Seeing the Lessons
1   Mama Never Gave Me a Doll   24
2   When the Side Effects Are Worse   31
3   Forgiveness Ain't for Suckers   38

Part Three: Navigating the Day to Day
1   Triple Your Salary in No Time   46
2   Peace Precedes Victory   53
3   Stay True to You   60

FORWARD

Each volume of this series was designed to build upon the knowledge and perspective introduced in its predecessor. This first volume encourages you to tackle the "chaos" so that you can create the mental and emotional room necessary to focus on "career". In the second volume, we will discuss concrete actions that you can take to advance your career and/or embark on your entrepreneurial endeavors. In the final volume of <u>The Guide to Balancing Chaos & Career</u>, your attention will be directed toward exploring the most effective ways to handle life after achieving success.

It is my hope that you will leverage the perspective and techniques I offer in this collective series as a toolkit to reference when navigating the complexities of those real-life situations that occur in the midst of climbing the corporate ladder. Most importantly, by reading this work, you should find yourself becoming more strategic about your personal journey toward success.

HOW TO USE THIS GUIDE

Each page of this guide is followed by a journal entry that allows you to apply the scenarios being discussed to your own life. Four writing prompts help expand and stimulate your thinking:

1. This reminds me of
2. I wish I would have
3. Now I want to
4. When I finish this chapter, I will

By making the reading interactive, the guide moves out of abstraction and becomes more personal, increasing your commitment to the changes and ideas presented in the text.

I encourage you to always write something under each prompt, even if it doesn't relate directly to the specific prompt. Chronicling your thoughts and progress on a consistent basis will help kindle the thinking that leads to real change and self-improvement.

Once you have read the complete guide for the first time and left responses under each prompt, the guide transforms into a personal action plan. Use your plan to help you conquer new heights in your journey toward the best you!

Part 1:

Making the Decision

Section Goals:	
1.	Determine that your life is worth living despite the chaos
2.	Decide to embark on the path toward self-improvement

Chapter 1: The Big Vent

Virtually every day our news outlets and feeds seem to be swamped with depressing headlines. From mass shootouts and non-violent-protests-gone-violent, to natural disasters and not-so-presidential behavior. Our senses and emotions are overwhelmed with seemingly infinite amounts of negative imagery and discourse. Yet and still, we are expected to continue about our days as if nothing

This reminds me of:

_____
_____
_____
_____
_____
_____

I wish I would have:

_____
_____
_____
_____
_____
_____

Now I want to:

_____
_____
_____
_____
_____

When I finish this chapter I will:

_____
_____
_____
_____
_____
_____

happened. Most of us could not call off work because we are emotionally distressed by the latest shooting of an unarmed Black man we've never met. Assignments don't get postponed because a hurricane or earthquake has destroyed the lives of hundreds of our brothers and sisters in neighboring states and countries. We are expected to be just as diligent, work just as hard, and smile just as often, regardless of the compounding pain inside our hearts.

To my boss: At one point in time, you were in my shoes. This does not mean that the position you now hold enlightens you to a

This reminds me of:

_____
_____
_____
_____
_____
_____

I wish I would have:

_____
_____
_____
_____
_____
_____
_____

Now I want to:

_____
_____
_____
_____
_____
_____

When I finish this chapter I will:

_____
_____
_____
_____
_____
_____

degree of infallibility. My contributions are valid and my perspectives are just as essential to this firm as yours. Help me, teach me, learn from me. Discouraging me by stifling my opinions and rushing my production will only hurt us both in the end. Give me the autonomy and respect I need to do me and we all will benefit.

To my teachers: Test scores are not adequate measures of my character nor are they the best reflections of my potential. You are here to enlighten, uplift, and encourage. Some of you understand this and do exceedingly well with reaching your students because of it. When my education is so closely

This reminds me of:

_____

I wish I would have:

_____

Now I want to:

_____

When I finish this chapter I will:

_____

interconnected to the opportunities I will have in my future, it is the educator that shouldn't mistake their unique position in this delicate equation with an opportunity to oppress.

To my friends: Life's journey is full of stressful events. If there are things or people that bring you chaos and distract you from your career, why not cut them lose? By exercising your restraint in areas that you have control over, you are able to free up your mental and spiritual energy to battle those chaotic events that occur outside of your realm of control. Toxic friendships are not only defined by the presence of negative

This reminds me of:

_____
_____
_____
_____
_____
_____

I wish I would have:

_____
_____
_____
_____
_____
_____
_____

Now I want to:

_____
_____
_____
_____
_____
_____

When I finish this chapter I will:

_____
_____
_____
_____
_____
_____
_____

*characteristics (i.e. arguments, jealousy, disloyalty, etc.) but can also include those relationships that allow friends to lull in mediocracy. That said, a **good** friend is invaluable for many of the same reasons. As you progress through life, you will find comfort and peace in those private conversations you share with your support system. Learning from each other's mistakes and successes helps to make you better people. Never mistake the need to meet a goal or allow the mass acquisition of wealth to serve as a replacement for those human interactions and bonds that are just as critical to your wellbeing. A good friendship is*

This reminds me of:

_____
_____
_____
_____
_____
_____

I wish I would have:

_____
_____
_____
_____
_____
_____
_____

Now I want to:

_____
_____
_____
_____
_____

When I finish this chapter I will:

_____
_____
_____
_____
_____
_____

a wonderful thing to find and an even more terrible thing to waste.

To my first heartbreak: Your loss.

To my rebound love: Sorry for placing undeserved expectations on you so quickly and diligently without your consent. I know this was more than you signed up for, which is why I'm releasing you back into the waters for which you seem to yearn. The space you occupied was never permanent despite how intimate our interactions. Your presence served a purpose, but your resistance reconstructed good intentions into bitter monologues. Yet I thank you still, for reviving

This reminds me of:

_____
_____
_____
_____
_____
_____

I wish I would have:

_____
_____
_____
_____
_____
_____

Now I want to:

_____
_____
_____
_____
_____

When I finish this chapter I will:

_____
_____
_____
_____
_____
_____

my flailing confidence and reassuring me that I still got it.

To my former friends: I never wanted to see our friendship come to an end, yet I'm still unable to find sadness in the fact that we're no longer friends. Thank you for memories filled with laughs and insiders. Thank you for the spare T-shirts and eyeliner you'll never get back. Everything I said to you during our friendship was sincere and I find peace in that. I know from time to time I'll hear a song that reminds me of you and probably get sentimental enough to want to reach out. But I won't. I appreciate the lesson that embodied itself in you, but I've learned it

This reminds me of:

_____
_____
_____
_____
_____

I wish I would have:

_____
_____
_____
_____
_____

Now I want to:

_____
_____
_____
_____
_____

When I finish this chapter I will:

_____
_____
_____
_____
_____
_____

and am moving on. I am prepared to experience new beginnings and fresh starts with people that have desire to learn from and teach me. My social growth is an important and significant part of my total development and I will not forego it for popular social constructs of loyalty. New friends represent new opportunities, not a deviation from some predetermined alliance. I wish you well and will cherish you from distances, hoping that the next time we happen to meet will be brief yet cordial.

To my parents: I know parenthood is tough and despite all the books out there, it's pretty much a learn-as-you-go sort of job. Life

This reminds me of:

___

I wish I would have:

___

Now I want to:

___

When I finish this chapter I will:

___

probably hasn't been everything you wanted it to be and you saw my birth as an opportunity for a redo. Just remember that I am here by no doing of my own and am doing the best I can with the hand I was dealt. As I grow older and the realities of life consume larger portions of my days, I sometimes let too much time elapse between calls. Sometimes, this is intentional. Sometimes, it's not. Still, know that I have not forgotten the lessons you've instilled in me.

This reminds me of:

_____
_____
_____
_____
_____
_____

I wish I would have:

_____
_____
_____
_____
_____
_____
_____

Now I want to:

_____
_____
_____
_____
_____
_____

When I finish this chapter I will:

_____
_____
_____
_____
_____
_____
_____

Chapter 2: Self-Blaming

Being successful is rarely a byproduct of luck. In order to get what you want, you work for it. This may or may not seem rudimentary, but when you reflect on and observe the growing number of ways people try to avoid the "work" element (i.e. gambling, sending chain letters on Facebook, etc.), sense starts to seem not-so-common after all. One of the many dangerous deceptions

This reminds me of:

_____
_____
_____
_____
_____
_____

I wish I would have:

_____
_____
_____
_____
_____
_____

Now I want to:

_____
_____
_____
_____
_____
_____

When I finish this chapter I will:

_____
_____
_____
_____
_____
_____
_____

prevailing in mainstream media today is the perpetuation of the "gold strike" mentality. We teach our kids to aspire to be athletes and musicians when the percentage of people who actually achieve financial success in those arenas is so negligible that if it was any other profession, we would do anything but encourage our children to take it up as a career. We teach college students to study hard so that they can become the new leaders of the world, without giving them the basic tools they need to function in real society. How many college seniors understand how to file taxes or even fill out basic new hire

This reminds me of:

_____
_____
_____
_____
_____
_____

I wish I would have:

_____
_____
_____
_____
_____
_____
_____

Now I want to:

_____
_____
_____
_____
_____

When I finish this chapter I will:

_____
_____
_____
_____
_____
_____
_____

documentation? We encourage adults to acquire massive amounts of debt (i.e. credit cards, mortgages, car notes, student loans, etc.) while working jobs that **trickle** money in their bank accounts all in pursuit of an "American Dream" that leaves the best part of the "dream" for the 65 and up years of retirement.

Needless to say, my definition of hard work is a little different. I believe that the traditional models of hard work were intentionally designed and propagated throughout generations to produce a society full of hamsters-in-a-wheel, with people spending their entire lives exerting

This reminds me of:

_____
_____
_____
_____
_____
_____

I wish I would have:

_____
_____
_____
_____
_____
_____

Now I want to:

_____
_____
_____
_____
_____

When I finish this chapter I will:

_____
_____
_____
_____
_____
_____

unnecessary amounts of time and effort doing the *chasing* and not the *getting*. If you were to exert that same energy into learning as much as you can about who you are, the world, and the role you desire to play in the larger scheme of things, you might be much better equipped for achieving success.

A quick Google search of "self-improvement books" will reveal thousands of titles from authors of all professions and walks of life. People are undoubtedly drawn to the idea of becoming better versions of themselves and often seek answers from those authors who appear to have

This reminds me of:

_____
_____
_____
_____
_____
_____

I wish I would have:

_____
_____
_____
_____
_____
_____
_____

Now I want to:

_____
_____
_____
_____
_____
_____

When I finish this chapter I will:

_____
_____
_____
_____
_____
_____
_____

something they want (money, fame, power, enlightenment, etc.). I'll go ahead and risk my credibility by sharing my opinion on the matter: the lion's share of self-improvement guidance is a load of crap. People spend way too much time consuming content created by other human beings who are just as unsure as the readers they aim to help. The time, **money**, and effort that a person spends listening to other people's good ideas on life is almost embarrassing. Because I have such a pessimistic view of books like mine, I will do my best to discourage you from taking my word as bond. This guide is not meant to

This reminds me of:

_____
_____
_____
_____
_____
_____

I wish I would have:

_____
_____
_____
_____
_____
_____
_____

Now I want to:

_____
_____
_____
_____
_____
_____

When I finish this chapter I will:

_____
_____
_____
_____
_____
_____

dictate your life, but to stimulate your own reflective thought process so that **you** will make the changes you determine are necessary to reach your goals.

Some "self-help" writers attempt to establish their credibility by convincing you that because they've found success they must know the answers for you. What worked for them must work for you too, right? While it is admirable for those who have figured things out for themselves to share their enlightenment with others, I disagree with the approach. No two people have identical sets of mental models informing their way of being; therefore, no

This reminds me of:

_____
_____
_____
_____
_____
_____

I wish I would have:

_____
_____
_____
_____
_____
_____

Now I want to:

_____
_____
_____
_____
_____

When I finish this chapter I will:

_____
_____
_____
_____
_____
_____

two people will have the same pathway to or definition of success. I encourage you to focus your energy on unveiling your own underlying motivations for seeking help. Then, harness that insight to define your *own* vision(s) of success and develop your *own* path to it. This guide was crafted to allow us to become partners in your discovery while allowing you to determine for yourself what application looks like.

This reminds me of:

_____
_____
_____
_____
_____
_____

I wish I would have:

_____
_____
_____
_____
_____
_____

Now I want to:

_____
_____
_____
_____
_____
_____

When I finish this chapter I will:

_____
_____
_____
_____
_____
_____

Chapter 3: Your Life is Worth Living

When I witness how talented and interesting other people appear to be I get disheartened. I try and ease my feelings of mediocracy by reminding myself that everyone can't be superstar athletes or discover cures for cancer...then who'd be there on the couch to keep those Netflix ratings up? Still, it's hard not to worry over your purpose when everyone around you (or

This reminds me of:

_____
_____
_____
_____
_____
_____

I wish I would have:

_____
_____
_____
_____
_____
_____
_____

Now I want to:

_____
_____
_____
_____
_____
_____

When I finish this chapter I will:

_____
_____
_____
_____
_____
_____
_____

at least all of the strangers in your newsfeed) appears to be winning at life.

My dating skills suck. It's pretty much a real-life enactment of the Urkel-Stefan transformation the moment I make eye contact. Needless to say, I'm single. Of course, I continue to keep hope alive and tell myself that one-day things will click into place. Yet and still, I've mentally crafted my "plan b" and thought of the names of all six dogs I'll get to fill my maternal void in 10 years. I also have established some seemingly borderline-unhealthy attachments to all my friends' and family members' kids.

This reminds me of:

_____
_____
_____
_____
_____
_____

I wish I would have:

_____
_____
_____
_____
_____
_____
_____

Now I want to:

_____
_____
_____
_____
_____
_____

When I finish this chapter I will:

_____
_____
_____
_____
_____
_____
_____

The common denominator of both of my complaints is that my center of focus is shifted toward things that are outside of my direct control, creating an "out there" mentality. We have to be cognizant of the ways in which we allow societal pressures and standards to rate where we are in our lives. Don't make it a habit to look to others and say, "I can do it too", rather, look within yourself and simply affirm "I can do it". In doing so, you recapture power over your life and your destiny. Re-center your locus of control to be internal. Work intentionally to rid your vocabulary of the common terminologies that shift your focal point to

This reminds me of:

_____
_____
_____
_____
_____
_____

I wish I would have:

_____
_____
_____
_____
_____
_____

Now I want to:

_____
_____
_____
_____
_____

When I finish this chapter I will:

_____
_____
_____
_____
_____
_____

some external or abstract force that functions outside of your jurisdiction.

If you do not possess the internal drive and dedication necessary to improve your circumstance, life will eat you alive. No matter how many books you read, songs you listen to, or Facebook posts you screenshot for yourself, you must be willing to look inside yourself to determine that your life is worth the effort. This understanding will be fundamental to your success, regardless of what your end goal might be.

Situations *will* occur throughout your life that will *seem* to throw you off course

This reminds me of:

_____
_____
_____
_____
_____
_____

I wish I would have:

_____
_____
_____
_____
_____
_____

Now I want to:

_____
_____
_____
_____
_____
_____

When I finish this chapter I will:

_____
_____
_____
_____
_____
_____

and distract you from the plans and goals you've made. This is an inevitable part of life. What is not inevitable is the impact those situations *actually* have. **You are the only person that can allow negativity to take root in your story.**

Caution: The following page contains a personal contract. You may use the contract template I have included here or build your own. By signing your own personal contract, you agree to complete this guide with the intent of implementing the changes you list in your journal entries.

_____ *was born with purpose. There has never been another living being in history quite like me. My mistakes are my favorite part of life, they build character and teach lessons that I have my whole life to learn. Bitterness and hurt are temporary feelings that have no home in my destiny. Other people's definitions of failure do not inform my own. I will repurpose every negative event and feeling into something better. My future is my own, not my parents', not my teachers', not my boss', not my lover's, not my enemies', not even my friends'. I will not let my past accomplishments limit my potential by instilling unwarranted sensations of contentment. Every day is a new opportunity to do what I didn't get to yesterday. Since every change I make in my life changes the world, my goal is to live to leave a legacy.* **My life is my stage and I choose to make it the best production anyone has ever seen.**

Signed,

_____

Part 2:

Seeing the Lessons

Section Goals:	
1.	Explore the role your upbringing has played in how you function in adulthood
2.	Embrace the difficulties of your journey
3.	Learn to gain empowerment from forgiveness

Chapter 1: Mama Never Gave Me a Doll

Our childhoods are laden with so many quirky memories that we might often find ourselves sitting back and wondering how in the hell we made it this far. I can recall at least five near death experiences I had before the age of 13- though I'll spare you the details. Besides making for good lunch room conversations and standup comedy material, I believe that a deeper look into any of these childhood

This reminds me of:

_____
_____
_____
_____
_____
_____

I wish I would have:

_____
_____
_____
_____
_____
_____
_____

Now I want to:

_____
_____
_____
_____
_____
_____

When I finish this chapter I will:

_____
_____
_____
_____
_____
_____
_____

memories, good or bad, can reveal <u>useful</u> truths about ourselves, our world, and our relationship to the people around us.

Seeing the lessons. When I was growing up, my mom never gave me Barbie dolls or the like. What might be even more surprising (or depressing, depending on how fond you are of dolls) is that it wasn't until a few months ago that I even realized this. Now you might think my mom was either extremely mean, cheap, or some sort of super-feminist. However, when I recall the subtle ways in which my mother chose to relay her life lessons to me, I am amazed, humbled, and most importantly, grateful. I

This reminds me of:

_____
_____
_____
_____
_____
_____

I wish I would have:

_____
_____
_____
_____
_____
_____
_____

Now I want to:

_____
_____
_____
_____
_____
_____

When I finish this chapter I will:

_____
_____
_____
_____
_____
_____
_____

know that to her, me being able to make my own decisions and have autonomy over my own life was the underlying lesson in every aspect of my upbringing. It wasn't that she never gave me a doll, it was that I never asked for a doll and she therefore did not *force* those stereotypical ideologies (i.e. girls play with dolls, boys play with toy cars) into mental models. Reflect on your past and write down some of the events you've never viewed as lessons in your writing prompt.

Interpreting life as lessons. I hate writing. Always have. In school, I cringed at the phrase "research paper" almost just as

This reminds me of:

_____
_____
_____
_____
_____
_____

I wish I would have:

_____
_____
_____
_____
_____
_____

Now I want to:

_____
_____
_____
_____
_____

When I finish this chapter I will:

_____
_____
_____
_____
_____
_____

much as I did to "group project". It wasn't that I didn't know how to spell or couldn't build a bomb outline in 10 minutes. When I think about it, the part that makes me most anxious is the mechanics of it all. Knowing when to put dashes versus semi-colons, thinking of different ways to say the same word, MLA versus APA, etc. The creativity quickly turns into apprehension then anger, followed by avoidance via procrastination and always ending in a panicked result printed sometimes within the same hour as the due date. Fast forward a few years and my first career-level job was acquired as a result of a well-

This reminds me of:

___

I wish I would have:

___

Now I want to:

___

When I finish this chapter I will:

___

written cover letter. My first major expression of myself to the world came in the form of *writing a book*, of all things. How is it that something I dreaded so much was the very thing that fueled such significant life events? Short answer: I interpreted the lesson.

Life's lessons come in all shapes and sizes. It is up to us to view every situation or circumstance we encounter as a lesson and learn from it what we can. *Applying* what we learn doesn't always have to be taking action. Indeed, sometimes the most powerful thing we will do in life will be to remain silent or still in times of temptation.

This reminds me of:

_____
_____
_____
_____
_____
_____

I wish I would have:

_____
_____
_____
_____
_____
_____

Now I want to:

_____
_____
_____
_____
_____

When I finish this chapter I will:

_____
_____
_____
_____
_____
_____
_____

Sometimes, the purpose of a lesson might be simply to inform your frames of reference and perspectives. Whatever the form, just be sure you are aware and taking note.

When the lesson is too tough to apply. Forgiveness is the only way you can live the life you were meant to live. If you do not forgive your past, your pain, and yourself, you will forever be captive to the feelings of defeat and depression that engulf those who pity themselves. None of us were meant to live perfectly, so why not embrace your inevitable imperfections and hurt and use them to fuel your passion and

This reminds me of:

_____
_____
_____
_____
_____

I wish I would have:

_____
_____
_____
_____
_____
_____

Now I want to:

_____
_____
_____
_____
_____

When I finish this chapter I will:

_____
_____
_____
_____
_____
_____

creativity in a productive way. Forgive, and if you can, forget. Preserve your energy for the things you have control over. If all else fails, write a book about it.

This reminds me of:
_____
_____
_____
_____
_____

I wish I would have:
_____
_____
_____
_____
_____
_____

Now I want to:
_____
_____
_____
_____
_____

When I finish this chapter I will:
_____
_____
_____
_____
_____
_____

Chapter 2: When the Side Effects Are Worse

Watching a commercial for any prescription almost always includes a jumbled auctioneering of symptoms that make the original condition sound not-quite-so-bad. Sometimes, we get so focused on shortcuts that we forget it is the *journey itself* that builds the character we need to handle the victory. How often we look for an easy way

This reminds me of:

_____
_____
_____
_____
_____
_____

I wish I would have:

_____
_____
_____
_____
_____
_____
_____

Now I want to:

_____
_____
_____
_____
_____
_____

When I finish this chapter I will:

_____
_____
_____
_____
_____
_____
_____

out, not realizing that the true beauty of life comes from the things we witness during the struggle. When we try to avoid the growing pains associated with our lived experience, we open ourselves up to side effects that can far outweigh the perceived benefit of instant gratification. Let your trials and tribulations fuel your growth. Even more, take some time to reflect on the life lessons that can be learned from the virtue of patience. Notice that I did not directly say to *be* patient, because that would be hypocritical of me. Nevertheless, think about what the act of practicing patience allows. It gives time for you to

This reminds me of:

___

I wish I would have:

___

Now I want to:

___

When I finish this chapter I will:

___

complete things. It offers space for growing from your mistakes. It affords you the opportunity to observe your surroundings and contemplate meaning. All of these attributes of patience can undoubtedly improve your quality of life. Develop an appreciation for them and proactively work to integrate these qualities into your everyday life.

Patience in the corporate setting can be a blessing and a curse. On one hand, you never want to be in a position where it's been 25 years since your last promotion if you're still answering phones and opening mail. On the other hand, many people will

This reminds me of:

_____
_____
_____
_____
_____
_____

I wish I would have:

_____
_____
_____
_____
_____
_____

Now I want to:

_____
_____
_____
_____
_____

When I finish this chapter I will:

_____
_____
_____
_____
_____
_____

be able to progress up the corporate ladder through years of diligent hard work and dedication. Understanding this balance and exploiting this relationship can be one of the most crucial things to your career. In any case, taking shortcuts robs your personal development.

Dodging difficult circumstances can distort our journey. While you should probably avoid walking on train tracks, you should still try to accept the inevitable truth that the path to success *will* include a few wrecks along the way. When the wrecks do come, try to keep your focus on your ultimate goal or plan. Some might find it

This reminds me of:

_____
_____
_____
_____
_____

I wish I would have:

_____
_____
_____
_____
_____
_____

Now I want to:

_____
_____
_____
_____
_____

When I finish this chapter I will:

_____
_____
_____
_____
_____
_____

wise to plan for these wrecks. For instance, if you know your car is 25 years old and you haven't gotten an oil change all year, you might plan for disaster and avoid being late by leaving earlier than you need to get to your destination. Likewise, if you know your job or industry is known for layoffs, you might learn a skill or trade that you can do to still make money and keep your lights on during the off season. Sometimes the wrecks are unforeseen, but a person with strategy is constantly equipping themselves to handle them when they occur.

Being in the land of plenty, Americans

This reminds me of:

_____
_____
_____
_____
_____
_____

I wish I would have:

_____
_____
_____
_____
_____
_____
_____

Now I want to:

_____
_____
_____
_____
_____
_____

When I finish this chapter I will:

_____
_____
_____
_____
_____
_____

are constantly sold on get-rich-quick schemes. While the thought of retiring early with millions in the bank is on everyone's wishlist, we have to think about the implications. What would we do with the money? Would we simply buy more things? Would we give money to charity? Most of us can easily fantasize about what we'd do as millionaires, but what we might not consider is the impact our financial freedom might have on our surroundings. Without your meaningful contributions, society is left less fulfilled. This is by no means meant to discourage you from seeking financial wealth. On the contrary, I

This reminds me of:

_____
_____
_____
_____
_____
_____

I wish I would have:

_____
_____
_____
_____
_____
_____

Now I want to:

_____
_____
_____
_____
_____
_____

When I finish this chapter I will:

_____
_____
_____
_____
_____
_____
_____

challenge you to begin thinking strategically *now* about your future plans for life after you've acquired the riches. Never allow your financial freedom to free you from your obligation to contribute your unique gifts and talents to society.

This reminds me of:

_____
_____
_____
_____
_____
_____

I wish I would have:

_____
_____
_____
_____
_____
_____
_____

Now I want to:

_____
_____
_____
_____
_____

When I finish this chapter I will:

_____
_____
_____
_____
_____
_____
_____

Chapter 3: Forgiveness Ain't for Suckers

At this point in our lives, every one of us has heard at one point or another that we have to forgive. Idioms like "forgive and forget"—or the pessimistic cousin "forgive but don't forget"—run rampant. But what does that mean? How do we apply that to our daily lives? What if we can't forgive? As people attempting to climb up the corporate

This reminds me of:

_____
_____
_____
_____
_____
_____

I wish I would have:

_____
_____
_____
_____
_____
_____
_____

Now I want to:

_____
_____
_____
_____
_____
_____

When I finish this chapter I will:

_____
_____
_____
_____
_____
_____
_____

ladder, it can also be difficult to easily correlate a topic we might have learned in Church to our professional life.

Strength in forgiveness. To speak about forgiveness, to some, brings up thoughts of submission and passivity. Attributes that are rarely equated to good business acumen. But the act of granting forgiveness is one of the most powerful things a person can do. By forgiving someone, you take back the feelings of control they had over your life. They are no longer able to fuel themselves with your hurt. The act of forgiveness requires such power and self-control, that only the

This reminds me of:

___

I wish I would have:

___

Now I want to:

___

When I finish this chapter I will:

___

strongest people are able to do it genuinely. When you allow yourself to hold on to the anger and distress that your offender caused, you weaken your character and detract from your purpose. Dedicating dialogue and mental space to revisiting the offensive comments or actions of others significantly undermines your work toward your goals.

Forgiveness in the workplace. When we think about forgiveness, we often associate it with personal situations (our significant others, our parents, our friends, etc.). However, it can be just as critical to our mental health and peace to be forgiving

This reminds me of:

___

I wish I would have:

___

Now I want to:

___

When I finish this chapter I will:

___

in the workplace as well. Coworkers, bosses, and others in our networks will sometimes offend us. Sometimes this offense is intentional, often times it isn't. Whenever you start to keep a tally of the various things your boss did or said that got under our skin, you are detracting from your goals. When you allow the mistakes and actions of coworkers to bother you, whether you mention it or not, you are detracting from your goals. Train yourself to be slow to anger in the workplace. *(*Spoiler alert: We will discuss various techniques you can use to do this in volume II).*

This reminds me of:

___

I wish I would have:

___

Now I want to:

___

When I finish this chapter I will:

___

What forgiveness says about you.

Forgiveness is not just about showing mercy to your offenders. When you forgive, you are reiterating your commitment toward self-love, inner-peace, and personal growth. To forgive someone, prompted or not, builds your character. It signals to those around you that you are serious about your goals, so much so, that you refuse to be distracted by the temptations of bitterness and retaliation. You are allowing your success to even the score. Rather you admit it or not, you also will feel much better about yourself when you forgive vs. seek revenge. You'll know that

This reminds me of:

___

I wish I would have:

___

Now I want to:

___

When I finish this chapter I will:

___

you exhibited strength that does not come natural to most and that you won't feel guilty later once your initial emotion has subsided. Displaying forgiveness says that you are part of an elite group of people who are able to do what the average person struggles to and often avoids.

The different faces of forgiveness.
Saying "I forgive you" to someone who has done you wrong is not the only way to forgive someone. In some cases, it might not even be the best way. Different circumstances require different iterations of forgiveness. Sometimes, to forgive someone might mean to leave them, other

This reminds me of:

_____
_____
_____
_____
_____
_____

I wish I would have:

_____
_____
_____
_____
_____
_____
_____

Now I want to:

_____
_____
_____
_____
_____

When I finish this chapter I will:

_____
_____
_____
_____
_____
_____

times it might mean to embrace them. Forgiveness is more of an art than a science and it is up to you to determine for yourself what it looks like for your offenders. In the end, as long as you've truly released the bind of hurt and/or anger such that the person no longer has control over your actions or emotions, you've won!

This reminds me of:

_____
_____
_____
_____
_____
_____

I wish I would have:

_____
_____
_____
_____
_____
_____
_____

Now I want to:

_____
_____
_____
_____
_____

When I finish this chapter I will:

_____
_____
_____
_____
_____
_____

Part 3:

Navigating the Day to Day

Section Goals:	
1.	Determine your plan for financial security
2.	Let inner-peace be your guiding compass
3.	Preserve your identity in the face of temptation

Chapter 1: Triple Your Salary in No Time

When it comes to our worth, who is responsible for setting that value? Is it our boss? Is it our peers? Most of us want to be fairly compensated, but what is "fair"? Who determines that standard? Regardless of what is common in your industry, department, position, etc., **you must be the guardian of your own financial profile**. No one else is going to care as sincerely about your income as you

This reminds me of:

_____
_____
_____
_____
_____
_____

I wish I would have:

_____
_____
_____
_____
_____
_____

Now I want to:

_____
_____
_____
_____
_____

When I finish this chapter I will:

_____
_____
_____
_____
_____
_____

can. But, in order to command the salary we want, you must first be valuable. What skills do you have that set you apart? What information about your company or industry do you know that no one else knows. What can you do just a little bit better than the person sitting next to you? What networks have you developed that can be leveraged? These are all key things you should be assessing internally on a regular basis. Once you start developing good answers, it might be time to take the next step: Ask for what you want.

When I was hired in my first job, I had no experience whatsoever in the industry

This reminds me of:

_____
_____
_____
_____
_____
_____

I wish I would have:

_____
_____
_____
_____
_____
_____
_____

Now I want to:

_____
_____
_____
_____
_____
_____

When I finish this chapter I will:

_____
_____
_____
_____
_____
_____
_____

let alone for the specific job I applied. I applied anyways and got the job. Once I was there for a while and got the hang of things, I quickly realized I was more than capable of doing more. So, I did. Once I asked for what I wanted and got what I asked for, I worked a little harder and became just a little more valuable. Then I asked for more. Whatever your "more" is, don't be afraid to ask for it but be sure you have done your part in professionally developing yourself to be worth the ask. If you don't know who or how to ask, leverage your network. If you don't have a network, Google it.

This reminds me of:

_____
_____
_____
_____
_____
_____

I wish I would have:

_____
_____
_____
_____
_____
_____
_____

Now I want to:

_____
_____
_____
_____
_____
_____

When I finish this chapter I will:

_____
_____
_____
_____
_____
_____
_____

By no means is earning a biweekly stipend the only way to achieve financial freedom. Nor do I promote it as the end-all-be-all for any life plan. I use the term salary in a very general sense to describe quality of life; because isn't improving our quality of like the desired result of generating income anyways? Most of us spend a great deal of time focused solely on acquiring money. So much so, that once we actually get it we spend it on unnecessary things which we had no intention on buying before we got it.

Having money can change a person's outlook on life, in more ways than one. This

This reminds me of:

_____
_____
_____
_____
_____
_____

I wish I would have:

_____
_____
_____
_____
_____
_____
_____

Now I want to:

_____
_____
_____
_____
_____

When I finish this chapter I will:

_____
_____
_____
_____
_____
_____

is why it is important for us to recognize this shortcoming as a very human response and develop habits that teach us how to plan for those influxes of funds, be they regular streams from salaries or those highly anticipated annual tax refunds.

So what strategy can you employ today that will guarantee your financial security? I don't know. What I do know is that if you adhere to these few major keys, you'll be better off than you were before reading this guide.

1. **Make the effort.** Waiting for someone else to realize how great you are before they hire you will most certainly lead to disappointment and an eviction notice. Before you can

This reminds me of:

_____
_____
_____
_____
_____
_____

I wish I would have:

_____
_____
_____
_____
_____
_____
_____

Now I want to:

_____
_____
_____
_____
_____

When I finish this chapter I will:

_____
_____
_____
_____
_____
_____
_____

swim you have to dip your toes in the water. Apply for that job. Start that business. Sign up for that training program. It doesn't have to be a **sure** thing, a **big** thing, or even the **right** thing (although I strongly urge you to make sure it's a **legal** thing).

2. **Diversify your efforts.** Putting your eggs in multiple baskets and seeing which ones hatch not only is a wise practice but also gives you an opportunity to learn new things about yourself and the world around you. I stop here to caution against the common misconception that being awake for 72 hours "chasing your dreams" is a sign you're working smarter. Self-care is central to obtaining and/or maintaining your inner peace, which is pivotal to your success.

3. **Multiply your efforts.** Once you've figured out something that works, either because it brings you income or because it's sparked some newly found passion of yours, do what you

This reminds me of:

___

___

___

___

___

___

I wish I would have:

___

___

___

___

___

___

___

Now I want to:

___

___

___

___

___

When I finish this chapter I will:

___

___

___

___

___

___

___

can to build upon that momentum. Magnify the impact of the change by spending more time on it, learning more about it, teaching others about it, etc. I'll also note here that waiting until you have more time is a surefire way to kill that momentum. Make time.

In the second volume, we will review this concept in much further detail. For now, you should maintain your focus on preparing yourself for the dedication and commitment that will be required to execute your plan.

This reminds me of:

_____
_____
_____
_____
_____
_____

I wish I would have:

_____
_____
_____
_____
_____
_____
_____

Now I want to:

_____
_____
_____
_____
_____
_____

When I finish this chapter I will:

_____
_____
_____
_____
_____
_____
_____

Chapter 2: Peace Precedes Victory

Peace of mind is the single most valuable thing there is. No matter how much money, power or respect you think you have, if you do not possess internal peace you will always be unsatisfied. Society teaches us all the ways of getting satisfaction through things, people, places, and other external factors. What they don't advertise is that true satisfaction will only come once you re-

This reminds me of:

___

I wish I would have:

___

Now I want to:

___

When I finish this chapter I will:

___

center your focus *away* from all of these things and *towards* an inner locus of control. There are plenty of books, religions and philosophical schools of thought that teach us ways to achieve inner peace. Here are a few easy and straightforward things you can start to do today to begin to build your own inner peace:

1. **Spend a few moments each day appreciating the little things.** For example, stare at the doors in your house and think about all the people that were able to feed their families because they were able to work in the plant that produced them. Stare at the dirty dishes in your sink and be grateful that in a world where the vast majority of people are experiencing food insecurity, you were able to enjoy that bowl of Ramen Noodles. Step outside to let the sun shine on your face and find appreciation in the fact that you can.

This reminds me of:
___
___
___
___
___

I wish I would have:
___
___
___
___
___
___

Now I want to:
___
___
___
___

When I finish this chapter I will:
___
___
___
___
___

2. **Save some you for yourself**! Every interaction with another human-being requires energy. Be mindful of who you allocate your energy to; if they aren't important to you then they should not be allowed in your words, thoughts, or actions. Gossip, promiscuity, and over bookings are an unsustainable way of life that will only push you further from your goals (unless of course you're aiming for that lifestyle, in which case: keep up the good work). The people you surround yourself with and give your energy to have significant impact on your well-being and even your future. Every decision you make today influences your life tomorrow, next month, next year, etc. Don't take it lightly!
3. **Keep it movin'**. Shit happens. Every, single, day. You can't allow it to consume you and knock you off track. People die, girlfriends cheat, jobs get lost, cars get stolen, etc. Of course, these things are heartbreaking, and you should absolutely take some time to mourn and allow the 7 Stages of Grief to run its course. But you must realize, and realize quickly, that these things are, always have been, and always will be a part of life. Being among the land of the living requires us to experience the good, the bad and the ugly. There's an old adage that says, "there's

This reminds me of:

_____
_____
_____
_____
_____
_____

I wish I would have:

_____
_____
_____
_____
_____
_____

Now I want to:

_____
_____
_____
_____
_____

When I finish this chapter I will:

_____
_____
_____
_____
_____
_____

nothing new under the sun." I can't tell you how invaluable this phrase was throughout my life as I experienced the ugly. Putting my struggles in perspective- that this is not the first or last time this has happened to someone, this is not the end of my story, brought unsurpassed peace to my world.

If you remember nothing else in this volume, remember these three points: **Your life can only be yours if *you* live it. Give yourself the chance to experience life and all its possibilities. Do not weigh yourself down with unnecessary *chaos*.**

Because life is so unpredictable, we have to put in work in order to build a stable foundation so that we can handle the waves as they come. Training your mind to repurpose every event into a teachable

This reminds me of:

_____
_____
_____
_____
_____

I wish I would have:

_____
_____
_____
_____
_____
_____
_____

Now I want to:

_____
_____
_____
_____
_____

When I finish this chapter I will:

_____
_____
_____
_____
_____
_____

moment is a great way to build this foundation. Learning from your mistakes requires a shift in thinking, from "this happened to me" to "this experience showed me". Further, any negative event that we do not repurpose into a lesson will be a waste. Don't miss out on your opportunities to learn and grow.

Allow yourself to fall and get back up to build character. Expose yourself to pain and failure *only if* you can make the commitment to learn from them. Otherwise, you are simply destroying yourself. Before we can improve our situations, we should be honest with

This reminds me of:

_____
_____
_____
_____
_____
_____

I wish I would have:

_____
_____
_____
_____
_____
_____

Now I want to:

_____
_____
_____
_____
_____

When I finish this chapter I will:

_____
_____
_____
_____
_____
_____

ourselves about our current predicament. Assess your current situation. Who do you talk to on a daily basis? What do you talk about? What places do you visit regularly? What physical, mental and spiritual activity do you engage in? What content are you consuming consistently? Now, ask yourself how all of these things are assisting you in reaching your goals. Are there some things missing? Are there some things you are doing that have no impact on the target you have in mind? What might you do to better align your actions and behaviors so that they reflect where you're headed? Repeat this exercise often to keep yourself on

This reminds me of:

___

___

___

___

___

___

I wish I would have:

___

___

___

___

___

___

___

Now I want to:

___

___

___

___

___

___

When I finish this chapter I will:

___

___

___

___

___

___

___

track, especially as unexpected events occur. This type of honest self-assessment begins to build the foundation you need to resolve those areas of cognitive dissonance that often are the source of disturbance for your inner peace.

This reminds me of:

_____
_____
_____
_____
_____
_____

I wish I would have:

_____
_____
_____
_____
_____
_____

Now I want to:

_____
_____
_____
_____
_____

When I finish this chapter I will:

_____
_____
_____
_____
_____
_____

Chapter 3: Stay True to You

A lot of times, we say want something, but we don't want to do what it takes to get it. In some cases, we allow ourselves to neglect our own values and self-esteem, thinking this is what defines a "go-getter". Any accomplishment you've achieved that required you to forgo your true identity was not an accomplishment. Mass media and other misinterpretations of success from society can embed our minds with so many

This reminds me of:

_____
_____
_____
_____
_____

I wish I would have:

_____
_____
_____
_____
_____
_____

Now I want to:

_____
_____
_____
_____
_____

When I finish this chapter I will:

_____
_____
_____
_____
_____
_____

false ideologies that, over time, it can become increasingly difficult to accurately distinguish between good and bad. It is up to us to guard our hearts, our minds, and our efforts. No one can be *you* but *you*, and without you, there is no one that can fulfill the void of your absence in society. This is why it is so important to not only be you and stay true to your identity, but to also work diligently to be the best *you* possible. There will only ever be one version of you to exist, so why not put your best foot forward and do all you can to outdo yourself! In the "Corporate America" landscape, it can be difficult to be yourself.

This reminds me of:

_____
_____
_____
_____
_____
_____

I wish I would have:

_____
_____
_____
_____
_____
_____

Now I want to:

_____
_____
_____
_____
_____

When I finish this chapter I will:

_____
_____
_____
_____
_____
_____

Tradition and unwritten rules flow heavily through conference rooms and cubicles. Depending on your role, you might find it extremely tempting to bite your tongue, even in those instances where you should be vocal. Learning how to get your point across and your opinions heard is a critical step in any career. You must make a conscientious effort to stick to your principles, despite the perceived risks of voicing them. No, I am not encouraging you to disrespect your boss or coworker at your next meeting. Being true to yourself means you don't compromise your beliefs, but it does not entitle you to be distasteful. It

This reminds me of:

_____
_____
_____
_____
_____
_____

I wish I would have:

_____
_____
_____
_____
_____
_____
_____

Now I want to:

_____
_____
_____
_____
_____

When I finish this chapter I will:

_____
_____
_____
_____
_____
_____
_____

also is not meant to encourage insubordination. To elevate or maintain your reputation as a person to be respected and heard, you must teach yourself to strike that delicate balance between assertiveness and tact.

Sometimes we tend to stifle our joy when those around us aren't having as good of luck. Don't be afraid to flaunt your happiness. This is not only unfair to ourselves, but even does more harm to those we are attempting to shield. You deserve to be delighted and should embrace those opportunities as they come. To deny yourself that experience only

This reminds me of:
_____
_____
_____
_____
_____
_____

I wish I would have:
_____
_____
_____
_____
_____
_____
_____

Now I want to:
_____
_____
_____
_____
_____
_____

When I finish this chapter I will:
_____
_____
_____
_____
_____
_____
_____

detracts light from the only bit of sunshine your downtrodden neighbor might witness that week.

That said, be mindful of your energy deposits. For people that view work as a distraction from what's going on at home, coming into the office to hear about your troubles robs them of this privilege. If you do have negative news you must share, try to only tell those who ask. The workplace should not be used as a venue for seeking counsel. *Do your best to deposit positive energy in your workplace.*

This reminds me of:

_____
_____
_____
_____
_____
_____

I wish I would have:

_____
_____
_____
_____
_____
_____

Now I want to:

_____
_____
_____
_____
_____

When I finish this chapter I will:

_____
_____
_____
_____
_____
_____
_____

WRAPPING UP

Now that you have come to the end of the first volume of this guide, take a few days to reflect on your journal entries. Before proceeding to the next series, it is important to allow yourself time to absorb and enact the concepts and plans you have encountered and made thus far. To be sure you get the most out of your experience, I recommend the following:

1. <u>Reread and reflect</u> on each comment you made under the "When I finish this chapter, I will" writing prompt.
2. <u>Draft an actionable plan</u> to implement these changes. Be sure your personal plan is concrete and commit yourself to executing it.
3. <u>Share what you've learned</u> with others. Ideally, the more enlightened your peers are, the less chaotic they'll become.

STAY TUNED...

So far, we've laid a solid emotional and mental foundation that will allow you to be most receptive to the next phase of your personal development plan. The second volume of <u>The Guide to Balancing Chaos & Career</u> will discuss concrete actions that you can take to advance your career and/or embark on your own entrepreneurial endeavors.

Stay Connected!

Scan this QR code to follow @chaoscareer on Instagram and receive important release date information for Volume II!

Questions/Comments?

balancechaoscareer@gmail.com

ABOUT THE AUTHOR

T.M.B. is a rising author from Detroit, Michigan with over a decade of experience in Corporate America and entrepreneurship. Before becoming a writer, she received a degree in Biochemistry & Molecular Biology from the College of Wooster, with a minor in Africana Studies. While writing this series, she also progressed through two Masters degrees in Business Administration and in Finance. By day, she works at one of the oldest philanthropic organizations in her city, where her writing helps ensure thousands of under-served individuals receive assistance each year. By night, she can be found volunteering in her community, coaching entrepreneurs, or launching another one of her own business ventures.